WRESTLING SUPERST★RS

SHEAMUS

BY BLAKE MARKEGARD

EPIC

BELLWETHER MEDIA • MINNEAPOLIS, MN

EPIC BOOKS are no ordinary books. They burst with intense action, high-speed heroics, and shadows of the unknown. Are you ready for an Epic adventure?

This edition first published in 2015 by Bellwether Media, Inc.

No part of this publication may be reproduced in whole or in part without written permission of the publisher. For information regarding permission, write to Bellwether Media, Inc., Attention: Permissions Department, 5357 Penn Avenue South, Minneapolis, MN 55419.

Library of Congress Cataloging-in-Publication Data

Markegard, Blake.
  Sheamus / by Blake Markegard.
    pages cm. – (Epic: Wrestling Superstars)
  Includes bibliographical references and index.
  Summary: "Engaging images accompany information about Sheamus. The combination of high-interest subject matter and light text is intended for students in grades 2 through 7"– Provided by publisher.
  ISBN 978-1-62617-145-9 (hardcover : alk. paper)
  1. Sheamus, 1978–Juvenile literature. 2. Wrestlers–United States–Biography–Juvenile literature. I. Title.
  GV1196.S45M37 2014
  796.812092–dc23
  [B]
                              2014002090

Printed in the United States of America, North Mankato, MN.

TABLE OF CONTENTS

WARNING!

The wrestling moves used in this book are performed by professionals.
Do not attempt to reenact any of the moves performed in this book.

THE DEBUT

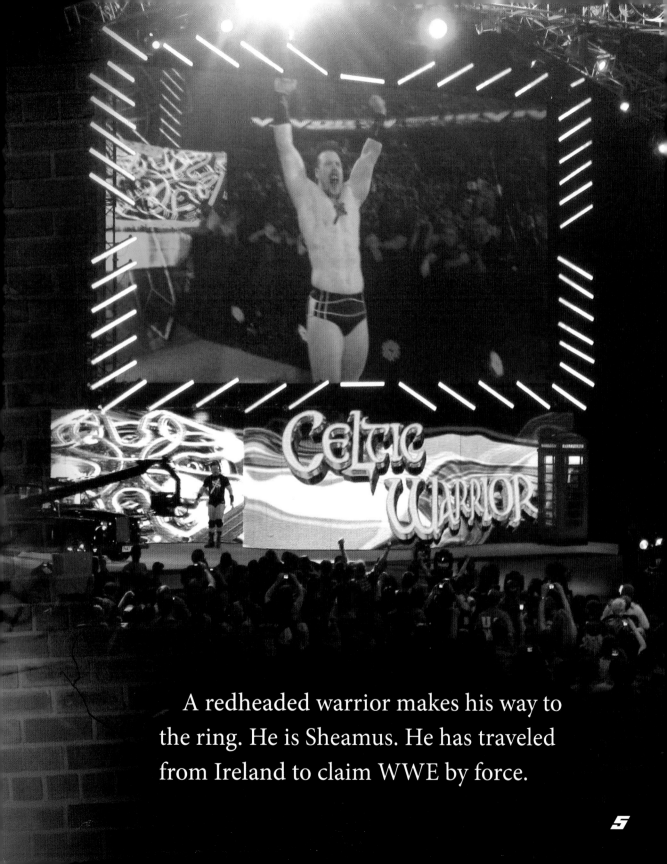

A redheaded warrior makes his way to the ring. He is Sheamus. He has traveled from Ireland to claim WWE by force.

Sheamus rushes into battle against
Oliver John. He **dominates** in his **debut**.
Soon Sheamus **pins** Oliver John on the
mat. His WWE takeover has begun.

UNSTOPPABLE

★

Sheamus declares that "not land, sea, or any other obstacle" can stop him.

WHO IS SHEAMUS?

Sheamus is a wrestler with fire in his belly. He is on a **mission** to **conquer** every WWE **title**. The **Celtic** Warrior believes he was born to fight.

LIFE BEFORE WWE

BIG ATHLETE

★

Sheamus played rugby and Gaelic football when he was young. These English and Irish sports are similar to American football.

Sheamus was born into a family of wrestling fans. As a kid, he dreamed of being a famous wrestler. He watched wrestling videos all the time.

Sheamus wrestled in small **leagues** in the **British Isles**. He became a star there. Soon he was ready to move to the United States.

BRINGING DISTRESS

★

In Europe, Sheamus was called SOS. This was short for his full wrestling name, Sheamus O'Shaunessy.

A WWE SUPERSTAR

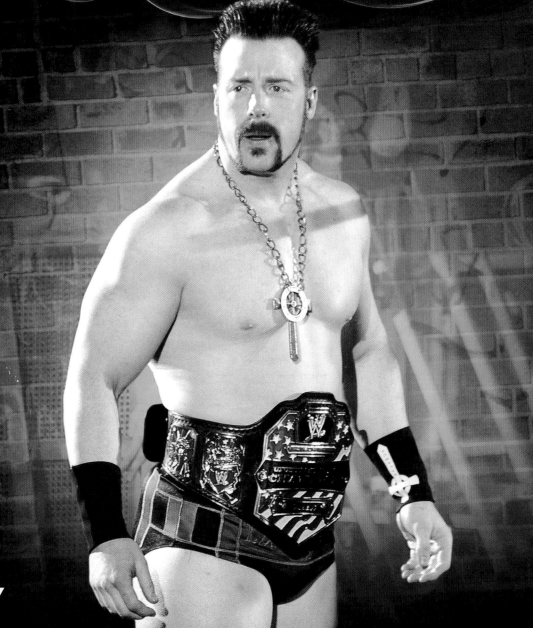

STAR PROFILE

WRESTLING NAME: Sheamus

REAL NAME: Stephen Farrelly

BIRTHDATE: January 28, 1978

HOMETOWN: Dublin, Ireland

HEIGHT: 6 feet, 4 inches (1.9 meters)

WEIGHT: 267 pounds (121 kilograms)

WWE DEBUT: 2009

FINISHING MOVE: Irish Curse

Fans did not like Sheamus when he first entered WWE. He went after John Cena and other fan favorites. However, he became more popular with every win.

In time, Sheamus changed from a **heel** to a **face**. In 2010, he won King of the Ring. He now rules WWE like he promised he would.

17

WINNING MOVES

Brave challengers usually
fall to the **Brogue** Kick.
Sheamus jumps in the air for
this **signature move**. Then
he kicks his opponent
in the face or chest.

BROGUE
KICK

19

Sheamus often puts an Irish **Curse** on his opponents. This **finishing move** begins with a lift. Then Sheamus slams his opponent down on his knee. What a backbreaker!

GLOSSARY

British Isles—Great Britain, Ireland, and the surrounding islands

brogue—a heavy shoe worn in Ireland

Celtic—relating to the Irish, Scottish, and other Celts

conquer—to overpower in order to gain control

curse—a cause of great harm or evil

debut—first official appearance

dominates—controls with the use of power

face—a wrestler viewed as a hero

finishing move—a wrestling move that finishes off an opponent

heel—a wrestler viewed as a villain

leagues—groups of people or teams united by a common activity

mission—a journey with a specific purpose

pins—holds a wrestler down on the mat to end a match

signature move—a move that a wrestler is famous for performing

title—championship

TO LEARN MORE

At the Library

Black, Jake. *WWE General Manager's Handbook*. New York, N.Y.: Grosset & Dunlap, 2012.

Black, Jake. *WWE Supersized Activity Book*. New York, N.Y.: Grosset & Dunlap, 2012.

Markegard, Blake. *John Cena*. Minneapolis, Minn.: Bellwether Media, 2015.

On the Web

Learning more about Sheamus is as easy as 1, 2, 3.

1. Go to www.factsurfer.com.

2. Enter "Sheamus" into the search box.

3. Click the "Surf" button and you will see a list of related web sites.

With factsurfer.com, finding more information is just a click away.

INDEX